WE'RE NOT ALL EQUAL: BECAUSE GOD SAYS SO

by

Donald Evchich

RoseDog Books

PITTSBURGH, PENNSYLVANIA 15238

RoseDog Books
585 Alpha Drive, Suite 103
Pittsburgh, PA 15238
Visit our website at www.rosedogbookstore.com

ISBN: 979-8-88527-913-0
eISBN: 979-8-88527-961-1

INTRODUCTION

This book has been written to Christians who believe Jesus Christ is the Son of God, and to those who do not believe, I hope it's an inspiration to them to know the <u>true love</u> of Jesus Christ, and the <u>false</u> love of Satan and his followers (Tares), Matthew 13:36-43. Evil deceives many by their subtle and <u>loving ways,</u> which are lies, which is their love but not the <u>truth,</u> and many fall prey to it. I pray this book will expound the truth of God's and Jesus Christ's love and their truth, which the World and its Tares cannot have (John 14-17) and the way through Christ Jesus and the Holy Spirit to discern between the two.

THEIR MEN HAVE BECOME LIKE WOMEN AND THEIR WOMEN LIKE MEN

The Democratic and Liberal parties who have Nancy Pelosi, Elizabeth Warren, Chuck Schumer, and Joe Biden as their leaders have been infected with the disease of reprobated minds. They have changed the natural use in which they were created into that which is against nature. Nancy Pelosi, Elizabeth Warren, and all the women that follow them are now wearing the jockstraps and Chuck Schumer, Joe Biden, and all their so-called men that follow them are wearing the tampons! Nancy and Elizabeth have become their own Jezebels (Revelation 2:20) and have transformed all the women that follow them into the spirit of Jezebel and the Spirit of whoredoms. It is written in Revelation 2:20-23, God's judgment will come on these women and their children. These women and so-called men who follow them that have the spirit of Jezebel in them must REPENT. Jesus says in Revelation 2:24-27, he will forgive them and put upon them no other burden.

As you read Isaiah 3:12, "As for my people, children are their oppressors, and women rule over them" (you can see what the colleges are producing today, women rule over them and these women will cause the people to err and to destroy their ways). These women are the filthy mindsets of the Democratic and Liberal parties who are written about in Hosea 4:12. The Spirit of whoredoms has caused them to err. In Jeremiah 51:30 the might of men fail and become like women, also in Jeremiah 50:37; Jeremiah 9:20; Isaiah 3:16-26; Isaiah 19:16; Proverbs 31:3; Ezekiel 13:17-23; Ezekiel 16:24, 38, 41; Ezekiel 23:45, 48; Nahum 3:13; Matthew 13:33; Matthew 16:6, 1, 12 (Jesus speaks of Leaven as doctrine, i.e. teachings); Mark 8:15; and 1 Timothy 2:10-15.

Many of you when reading this letter will be those who don't believe in many of the Bible's teachings. That's your choice, but at least you should acknowledge it as a history book on how nations of the world rose to greatness and what caused them to fall apart. <u>All that follow these women's so-called faith, which is a faith of the flesh and of reprobated minds have also murdered more innocent lives through abortions and selling baby parts for profit than all the men that were killed in the Revolutionary War to this very day, showing they can be more evil and vile than men have ever been.</u> These women and so-called men in the TV, media, news, and entertainment deserve the same judgment in their lives that God has promised on them in Revelation 2:22-23, and there is no respecters of persons in that judgment. These are the people that have turned the so-called melting pot of the United States into a garbage can and they are maggots that have multiplied to a great number, and their stink has risen to the heavens and the Lord God is about to judge them unless they repent.

If they choose not to, then the Lord God will allow the enemy to grow among you until they utterly destroy you by making you accept their teachings, laws, and lifestyles, and if you do not, then prison or death shall be your judgment. If Donald Trump is removed from where the Lord put him, then because of the filthy and wicked in this land, the Lord God shall and will remove himself from amongst the people and there shall be a gnashing of teeth. The Lord's judgment will start first with the people and churches that are so called by his name where the so-called ministers and leaders who have destroyed many of his flock with milk pablem teachings and have become lazy and laid back in their preaching in Spirit and Truth. They have become storytellers with no new revelations from the Lord because they all think that in their own righteousness (that so-called big number of believers) that these so-called men and women of the Democratic and Liberal parties are now passing laws that man can change their identity to be a woman and women can change their identity to men, and passing laws to have decent people forced to accept their filthy lifestyles. (2) Trigender bathrooms in schools so that young children can experiment with each other. (3) Boys acting like women and allowed to play in physical sports with women. And women allowed to play physical sports with boys and men, thus losing the gentleman relationship with women and women losing their ladylike relationship with men, thus becoming hostile toward each other. (4) Allowing men and women to come into America under the disguise of immigrants and bring in plagues and diseases without being tested and all out to go into any cities they desire or the Democrats send them to spread their diseases without ever being tested, and to have American leaders say they care about us and want

Americans to be vaccinated and wear masks but not for immigrants, who are in the hundreds of thousands who are allowed to run free in the United States to bring forth more diseases upon our nation, and because you filthy men and women and those who support your filthy minds. The Lord God will bring more sickness and plagues that the world has never known.

WHY THE N.I.V. BIBLE IS ONE OF THE WORST TRANSLATIONS AVAILABLE TODAY AND NOT PLEASING TO GOD

When the team of so-called Biblical Scholars met in 1965 to make a new translation of the Bible and invited many denominations to help them in their translation from United States, Great Britain, Canada, Australia, and New Zealand, they dazzled the people with their so-called knowledge of Greek and Hebrew, along with new scrolls found, new writings, vowel letters and vowel signs, and in 1973 the New Testament of the N.I.V. was published, but then they found out they had made many mistakes and had to make new corrections and revisions, and then they were added to the N.I.V. and it went into print in 1978. Then later again, they found out they had made more mistakes and again had to make more corrections and revisions and, finally again, put to print in 1983.

This clearly shows that these so-called Biblical Scholars were <u>not anointed by God, but</u> <u>anointed by</u> <u>man</u>. I will share with you what mistakes these scholars and Biblical translations still left uncorrected in 2007 that the Lord has showed me. (Remember this first.)

When God gave His Commandments and Laws to Moses, and had Moses write the first five books of the Bible, there's nowhere that Moses or any other prophet or man of God had to go back and correct the sayings that God gave them because of mistakes, because they were anointed by God, not man.

When you have to go back year after year and change the word of God that these scholars say they were called to do, it clearly shows God was not with them, but the Spirit of Error was (I John 4:6). When the first N.I.V. came out, 164 verses had been changed and altered, as well as omitting the name of our Lord God 169 times from the New Testament. Now there is another Bible called the New Translated, T.N.I.V., which has 3,686 inaccuracies in gender language. When I shared this new T.N.I.V. translation with the Christian leaders and scholars of the first N.I.V., their comments were that the writers of the T.N.I.V. were incorrect and had caved in to feminist pressures, which is no different than you bringing in your N.I.V. and having the churches, Christian leaders, and Christian people cave in to your pressure. The people who wrote the T.N.I.V. stand behind their interpretation of Greek, Hebrew, scrolls, writings, and vowel letters and vowel signs. Perverted as these writers are, the N.I.V. scholars are no different, for you both follow the Spirit of Error. There are many Scriptures that I could write to show the N.I.V. scholars of their ignorance of God's Word, but the one that is used very much by the N.I.V. readers is I Corinthians 13:10, 13, the so-called Love Chapter.

We first must establish what love is. We read in I John 4:8: "He that loveth not knoweth God; For God is Love." Since the N.I.V. people took Charity out of the

Bible, I asked a church member who had only N.I.V. Bibles in their pews, does your Church give help to the poor and needy? He answered, "Yes; we are a very charitable people." Then I told him that he and his church were not charitable people, just loving people. He then said, "We are both loving and charitable." He was then told they can't be charitable, because that word has been stricken from his N.I.V. Bible and cannot be found anywhere. I also told him that <u>Charity</u> - is an act of Good Will, a voluntary giving of money or other help to those in need. <u>Love</u> - is an expression of a deep and tender feeling of affection or attachment or devotion to a person or persons. <u>Charity</u> - is the outward giving of help or assistance to one in need. <u>Love</u> - is the inward feeling for a person. I have known many Christians who have said, "I love my brethren and pray for them, but I just can't help them at this time, but I love them" (<u>inwardly love</u>). Also, there are those Christians who love with their heart but not giving with their substance.

Charity is a gift of God's love, but to omit Charity and just put Love, then you must also put Love in place of grace, mercy, forgiveness, and all the gifts that come from the Father, which would make His word confusing and He is not the author of confusion. For by removing Charity from Scripture, and calling it the Love Chapter and it has already been established that God is Love, then we must say, <u>Love is Hate</u> (Malachi 1:3).

The Lord says he loved Jacob, but <u>hated</u> Esau. Revelation 2:6 and 15, the Lord <u>hates</u> the teachings of the Nicholations, Hosea 9:15, God says because of their wickedness, I <u>hate</u> them and will no longer love them. <u>Love is Anger</u>. Numbers 12:9, the <u>anger</u> of the Lord burned against them. Psalms 7:6, Arise O Lord in your anger, Mark 3:5, Jesus looked around at them in <u>anger</u>. <u>Love is Wrath.</u> Isaiah 13:9: the day of the Lord is coming, a cruel day with <u>wrath</u> and fierce anger. John 3:36, but whoever rejects the son will not see life, for <u>God's wrath</u> remains on him. <u>Love is War</u>, Exodus 15:3 and Revelation 19:11. <u>Love is Jealous</u>, Exodus 20:5: for I the Lord your God am a <u>Jealous</u> God. II Corinthians 11:2, Paul tells you he has a <u>Godly</u> jealousy (so if the N.I.V. interpreters are going to say Love is patient, Love is Kind, it does not envy, it does not boast, it is not proud, it is not rude, it is not self-seeking, it is not easily angered, it keeps no record of wrongs (which is untrue; <u>God's Love</u> keeps a record, Rev. 20:11-15), all are judged who did not take part in the first resurrection, for many so-called believers that were left behind will be saying, "Lord, Lord, did we not prophesy in your name, drive out demons and perform many miracles? Then will I tell them, I never knew you. God keeps a record of all your deeds, some will get crowns, others will be separated from God. (For all repented sins and secret sins will be judge out of His books). Love does not delight in Evil, rejoices with truth. It always protects, always trusts, always perseveres. So, if these N.I.V. interpretations are of Love, then they must also put in God's love is HATE, ANGER, WRATH, WAR, and JEALOUSY. But, the N.I.V. just feeds milk to the people with no meat. The N.I.V. tells you in Proverbs 10:12, <u>Love covers</u> over <u>all</u> wrongs. But, they then tell you in I Peter 4:8, <u>Love covers</u> only a <u>multitude</u> of sins. This again shows the Spirit of Error of these so-called scholars and theologians. I say to the N.I.V. writers, "Cleanse your hands, ye sinners, and purify your hearts, ye double minded; ye have opened the door to every kind of devilish Spirit to write its own Bible," just like the writers of the T.N.I.V. Bible, which many of you will be held accountable for.

Remember this well, Church, when you quote I Corinthians 13:1-13 and then Galatians 5:22 and 23, the Fruits of the Spirit, unless these fruits of the Spirit are established in truth they are meaningless, for the world can love one another, have joy, peace, gentleness, goodness, mercy, forgiveness, meekness, and temperance, but they cannot have the Truth, Love, they can have. For it is written in John 15:19 that the world has its own kind of love and does love its own. The world cannot receive the Spirit of Truth, because it neither sees him, nor knows him. John 14:17: But again, the world has its Love, but cannot have the Truth. We are not sanctified in Love; we are sanctified in the truth. John 17:17, and must worship the Father in Spirit and Truth. John 4:23 and 24: Jesus did not say love, which he could have, he said Spirit and Truth.

(Sanctified: "to make free from sin, purify to set apart us holy") For Satan himself will come preaching his worldly love, since he is the Ruler of this World. He showed Jesus all the kingdoms of the World and told Him he would give all these to Him if He would worship him. Jesus never said they were not his to give. So, as God is Love, Satan copies Love, but he can't have the Truth.

Recently, I received a letter that was sent to me on "Why I do not think the King James Bible is the Best Translation Available Today," written by Daniel B. Wallace, Ph.D. I will shortly be writing a response to his errors and worldly wisdom. The letter heading will be titled "Christian Pharisees in America and the World." So, if any Christian reads this man's writings, remember, he sincerely believes what he has written, but he is so sincerely wrong. The summary of this message that the Lord has given me is that if you don't have the King James Bible side by side with the N.I.V. or any other so-called Bible, you will pay the price for disobedience. Satan does not want the Christians to have the King James Bible next to any of those other unanointed Bibles, for then you shall clearly see their error. Recently, I received the Expositors Study Bible from Jimmy Swaggart Ministries, though I disagree with some of his teachings, what he did in writing this Study Bible is very acceptable. He did not change the King James Version, but then he gives his translation of Scripture next to the K.J.V. This, if every so-called Bible scholar did that it would be acceptable to the Lord. Since he would not be changing the word or adding to it, but, giving his own translation, which the people who read and study can accept or reject it. When God sent His word in the King James Bible to America in its early birth, and though there were other Bibles used, the King James Bible was used as the foundation and cornerstone which this country was built on.

Now Daniel B. Wallace, Ph.D., tells God in America's beginning, "God, you did not give us your best, so now that I have a Ph.D. will clean your word up for you, because many of the people could not understand the way that you had your word written."

When Christ calls for His Church, and you are reading the N.I.V. or any other Bible without the K.J.V. alongside, you shall and will be left behind.

If any who reads this message wants to know some of the other 164 verses omitted, or changed, ask and thou shall receive.

OBAMA: WHO AND WHAT??

What does Obama stand for and believe?

1) On a TV show, the interviewer George Stephanopoulos asked Mr. Obama what faith was he a believer of and associated with. Mr. Obama immediately said, "Muslim," which then Mr. Stephanopoulos said, "Don't you mean Christian?" then Mr. Obama said, "Oh, yeah, that's right, I'm a Christian." Wake up, people of America, this man is either speaking the truth or lying. The first words to come out of his mouth were true, he is a Muslim! The second words that came out of his mouth were a lie, that he was a Christian. You cannot be a Christian and sign a bill as senator that it is alright to put a child to death that has been born outside the mother's womb. But, you can do it easily if you are a Muslim, because your Bible, the Koran, tells you all that are outside the Muslim faith are infidels and any Muslim that puts infidels to death is guaranteed Paradise. Wake up, America! The enemy is already among you.

2) Omar Kudafy, who is the leader of Libya, has said that Obama was brought into the Muslim faith as a young man, and once you take the oath of being a Muslim, the only way out is eventual death.

3) The Nazi party proclaimed Hitler as their Messiah, and now the Democratic Party is claiming Mr. Obama as their Messiah and have even stooped so low as comparing him to Jesus as a peacemaker and doer of good works. When did Jesus ever agree to put any child inside or outside of the womb to death? Obama signed a statement to start sex education in schools, starting with kindergarten, and it's not to allow the children to know only about sexual predators, like the uneducated and ignorant news commentators on MSNBC and CNN said, but to teach kindergarten children to accept the homosexual alternate lifestyle and same-sex marriages, which would eventually destroy their young lives.

4) Obama has been in the presence and fellowshipped with Louis Farrakan, who is a Muslim who talks about Jesus. Obama is a so-called Christian, who talks about Jesus, but is a Muslim. And since the Koran justifies lying to achieve their alternate goal, Obama can lie with a straight face and be comfortable in it. Obama has been in the company and fellowshipped with William Ayres, who made a statement that the

bombings he did on the U.S. Capitol and the Pentagon were not enough, he should have done more. Obama also has fellowshipped and kept company and fellowship with rapper Ludacris, whose mouth is a sewer of perversions and filth. Obama is in the company and fellowship with his preacher friend Rev. Wright and said he didn't agree with his statements on damning America like militant Muslims do or for his racist statements, and then say after being in his church for 20 years, he didn't know all what this man stood for. A person would have to be blind, deaf, and dumb to believe him and sad to say millions do.

This is a true saying, you know the man by the company he keeps!

Obama and his relationships with "Hollywood," which is a cesspool, destroying our children, Obama drinks from the same "cesspool" cup that Hollywood does.

In conclusion, I pray that the people will open their eyes to the truth about this man, and not listen to the news media and its commentators and writers who for the most part are uneducated and ignorant in the Truth. But, because of their own personal goals and corrupt minds, they say what they report is for the betterment of the citizens that they care for. It is truly sad to see people that are turned over to believe their own lies. The only reason the Democrats want Obama is because they do think he is a god and he supports their Marxist and socialist agenda. And now he wants to become leader of the United Nations so he can dare his own army to enforce his agenda on the nations.

Remember this well, when you teach children sex education and the homosexual style of living, which is the main purpose of sex education, you embrace the spirit of whoredoms, which sexually will destroy a nation (Hosea 4:6-12).

WE ARE NOT ALL EQUAL

One of the most predominant sayings in the churches and more frequently used by the world and the Tares is that <u>we are all created equal</u>, which <u>is completely untrue</u>. Abraham Lincoln and Martin Luther King Jr. were both great leaders of this country, Lincoln in government and King in religion and civil rights, but were both wrong. Not because I say so, but because God the Father says so. In Ezekiel 18:25-32, the people of the Lord complained that the way of the Lord was not equal to them, and the Lord answered: "Hear now house of Israel; is not <u>My way equal</u> and not <u>your ways unequal</u>?" (Ez. 18:25). In verse 29, the people say the Lord is not equal again, the Lord answers a second time: "Are not my ways equal? <u>Are not your ways unequal</u>?" This does not mean that the people are all equal under the law like many preachers and so-called Biblical scholars say. The Lord would have said under His Law if He meant under the law, <u>but He meant your ways</u>.

The Democrats and Liberals who are the tares of this country, America, go to their ways of killing babies, selling their body parts to support their filthy elections, supporting you men having to have anal and oral sex with each other, young women having sex with each other, children in schools to have gender-neutral bathrooms, which will only lead to sexual assault and the children when left alone in the bathroom to sexually experiment with each other.

Now that the Democrats and Liberals are legalizing marijuana, saying its only for medical purposes to help young and old people cope with their illness, so will crack and heroin, you idiots. This law is being pushed through the country because many of the doctors, lawyers, and politicians are smoking and they don't want to get caught with it in their possession. So the tares are using their ways by making it a law to be used as a medical and recreational drug to cover up their addiction and the foolish and ignorant people support them. Now the country will have to put up with not just drunk drivers, but drug addicts on our highways, bringing more death to innocent people. What happened to the health slogan that smoking is bad for your health, but now smoking pot is alright?

No Democratic Liberal or tare is equal to a true Christ follower, who follows the Lord in Spirit and Truth. Though they might profess being a Christian, yet they are only counterfeit Christians who will never see the Lord's kingdom unless they repent. This Scripture, Deuteronomy 7:6: "For thou art a holy people unto the Lord thy God: thy God hath chosen thee to be a special people unto Himself, <u>above all people that are upon the face of the Earth,</u>" is only for the Lord's true believers who worship in Spirit and in Truth, not for the counterfeit Christians. This truly shows that the world and its people are not equal to the <u>Lord's true people</u>, but we are <u>special, not equal, but</u>

above all people upon the face of the Earth. Yet we are still a servant to those who want to hear the Truth. Those who don't, we kick their dust out of our shoes (Mark 6:10-13).

Nancy Pelosi, Chuck Schumer, and Andrew Cuomo, and the tares that follow their wicked and perverse ways are the children of the Devil, which we read in Matthew 13:30-43 and their birth in Psalms 58:3-11: "The wicked are estranged from the womb and they go astray as soon as they are born, speaking lies," which fits these people and their followers to a tee. It is written in Psalms 7:11: "God judges his righteous and is angry with the wicked," Pelosi, Schumer, Cuomo, and all tares every day.

So to believe we are all children of God is untrue, we are all part of His creation but because of our ways and free will, many choose to follow Satan, who was rebellious against God and was cast down to the Earth and destined for the Lake of Fire, and all those who follow him in sin, and his children, the tares. We were never born equal because the Lord God says so and not some men who sincerely meant well, but are sincerely wrong. We are entitled to life, liberty, and the pursuit of happiness, but not equal. We read in Matthew 4:8-9, the Devil showed Jesus all the Kingdoms of the World, and told Him he would give them all to Him if He would fall down and worship him. Jesus never said the Kingdoms of the world were not His, for He knew they were His from the day Satan and his followers fought against Michael the archangel and they were cast out of Heaven into the Earth having great wrath and Satan set up in his spiritual kingdom in the Earth, which is called the World. Thus it is written, if you love the World, you make yourself an enemy of God.

Christians are just pilgrims passing through, taking the Lord's Word to those who have an ear to hear. Remember, God is a wall builder, which we read in the book of Nehemiah, where He had Nehemiah build up the wall around Jerusalem. Then there is the most important and biggest wall the Lord built when He brings down from Heaven His Kingdom to His people in Revelation 21:1-27. The city has a height that is 12,000 furlongs high, which is 1,500 miles high, and the wall is 216 feet high and all tares, including Chuck Schumer, Nancy Pelosi, Andrew Cuomo, and all MSNBC and CNN personnel who support their agenda, will receive the judgment of Revelation 2:18. There shall be no respect of persons in that judgment. I tell those foolish pastors and ministers who say they don't build walls, they build bridges, there is nowhere in the Bible, God's Word, that He builds bridges, but He does build walls. Listening and following these stupid and ignorant people who want bridges and not walls against lawbreakers only shows their ignorance.

Finally, there is Barack, the traitor, Obama, who is a bigger traitor to this country than Benedict Arnold ever was. When he gave billions of dollars to Iran, his brother Muslims, which they used the money to outfit and supply the Muslims fighting against and killing our American soldiers. Since the leader of Iran has vowed to destroy America, this traitor Obama invited the brotherhood of Muslims to Washington, D.C., twice, to break bread with them while our soldiers were being killed in the battlefield. I believe he let them know that he, Chuck Schumer, Nancy Pelosi, and the Democratic Party would be sending them billions of American dollars to support them in their cause, fighting against our soldiers. What do you think would have happened to President Roosevelt after the Japanese bombed Pearl Harbor, that he would have invited the Japanese over to the White House to break bread with them and gave them millions of American dollars? Barack, the traitor, Obama deserves the same judgment Benedict Arnold received, but much stiffer. All those people, and the Democrats who supported him, are guilty of the deaths of the American soldiers that American money was used to kill them.

These Democrats and Liberals will give billions of American dollars to Iran, who vowed to destroy America to kill our soldiers, but nothing to build a wall to protect American people from drug dealers, rapists, murderers, and terrorists who disguise themselves as immigrants. These Democrats are the true traitors of this country.

INTERRACIAL MARRIAGE OR MATING

Since the beginning of man's fall from grace in the Garden of Eden and he was cast out, God colored the people's skin as they multiplied on the Earth to keep them separate and unto themselves, and each race was cursed with its own sicknesses and diseases, man still would not obey God's order of staying within their own kind. For it is written, "and when men began to multiply on the face of the Earth and daughters were born unto them, that the sons of God saw the daughters of men that they were fair, they took them wives of all which they chose" (Genesis 6:1, 2). "The Lord regretted that He had made man on the Earth and it grieved Him at His heart" (Genesis 6:6). Everything God created was separate and unto its own. God never mixed and mingled any part of His creation, for it is written, "And God created great whales and every living creature that moveth, which the waters brought forth abundantly, <u>after their kind</u> and every winged fowl after his kind and God saw that it was good. And God said, 'let the Earth bring forth the living creature <u>after his kind</u>'; cattle and creeping thing and beast of the Earth <u>after his kind</u>; and it was so. And God made the beast of the Earth <u>after his kind</u>, cattle after their kind and everything that creepeth upon the Earth <u>after his kind</u> and <u>God saw that it was good</u>" (Genesis 1:21- 25).

God did not create the yellow canary to mate with the red cardinal, nor did He make the white dove to mate with the black crow, nor did He have the seed of the rose mingle with the seed of a dandelion, and the list can go on forever. I only hope and pray you see that <u>God is not the author of confusion.</u> The Devil has been very successful in using men to mix seeds of flowers and animals all in the disguise of advancement and technology to make people believe it is all for their betterment. For it is written, "Lo, this only have I found, that God hath made man upright; but they have sought out many inventions" (Ecclesiastes 7:29). "Thus they provoked Him to anger with their inventions; and the plague brake in upon them" (Psalm 106:29).

Since man's fall in the beginning, Satan has been very successful throughout history in having men and women of different races have sex and mixed children through wars, and just plain lust. Satan knows God's plan and order to keep the races separate, that is why he is continually making people lust for one another, all in the name of love, but it is <u>his</u> so-called love, <u>not God's.</u> We can all be one people in the Lord in His body, but we don't mix the fingers with the toes or put our ears where our eyes are. Every race can be a part of the Lord's body, as every part of the body is different unto itself so must we be. And as being one body in the Lord, but each part different and unto itself, so are the races, one body in the Lord, but separate unto themselves.

In Ezra 9:1 we read about God's disapproval with marrying and taking strange wives. For it is written,

"We have trespassed against our God and have taken strange wives of the people of the land" (Ezra 10:2). The word strange is threefold: 1) different language, 2) different religious beliefs, and 3) different races. It is not just different religious beliefs, like many blind so-called religious scholars claim. A person's different religious belief does not totally make him strange, but his color and language do. If you saw a purple-and-green man walking down the street speaking in a language you never heard before, you would definitely think him strange. But, if you saw a man praying to a tree or animal, you would not think him as strange as the purple-and-green man.

In Nehemiah 13:23-26, you read again where God's men angered God by taking and marrying wives of different tongues, races, and beliefs and God cursed them. Even Solomon did sin by spreading his seed among different women of his concubines. The same God that was angry then is angered at the people of today who are called by His name and telling God to His face, "You were wrong, God, when you colored and separated the races, and we are going to correct your mistake."

Every race has its own curses of sickness and disease and when you interracially marry and have children, you spread the diseases of one race with the sicknesses and diseases of another race and thus the children became cursed by being carriers of the diseases of two races, and the more they interracially marry the more diseases come into the world. There are many examples, but I will only give you two. The white race came into America and brought with them chicken pox and measles, which destroyed many of the Indians, who never had the disease before. When the black race came to America, they brought sickle cell anemia, which was new to the white race. When the white and red race got married and had children, they brought their diseases to their children, their children continued it on. When the black and white race had children, so did the same things happen to them, their children as well as the yellow race.

When you mix all the diseases and sicknesses that are in the races and have children, they bring new sicknesses and diseases, which were never heard of before because you have mingled one disease with another, thus producing a new and different disease on you, your children, and others. To those who are already interracially married, because of blind and foolish teachers telling them that it was okay, ask God for forgiveness and if in your heart you are truly sorry, He will forgive and guide you in His word. But, if you believe what you did was right by interracially marrying, then you will be held accountable for telling God that He was wrong in coloring and separating the races, which only will lead to eventual heartache to you and your children. For obedience is worth more than anyone's sacrifice.

Being reborn in Christ does not give you the right to interracially marry, you are still under God's order. All churches that promote interracial marriage truly deserve God's curses on them, for you shall reap what you sow. When you see the people of the world embrace this act and call it love, that is not the love of God, it is the love and lust of the flesh, which continually wants to be disobedient. For if you follow the world and its love, the love of the Father will not be in you no matter how much you say it is!

People lose their heritage and birthright when they marry into different races, which is against God's order, and the children always suffer for it. There are many examples, but since the black-and-white examples are more obvious than all the others are, I pray that you will be able to see the truth.

Remember this well, God loves all, if they have accepted His son Jesus Christ, no matter what race or nation, as long as through obedience they stay in their own kind. When a black man or woman marries a white man or woman, if the white man or woman has blond hair and blue eyes, the children they have with the black man or woman will not have white skin, blue eyes, or blond hair. Their child will take on the looks and coloring of the black race, thus losing their heritage that God gave them. When men or women marry and have children outside of their own race or nation, it only shows that the men are <u>ashamed and not content with the women of their own race</u>. They will call it love, but in God's eyes it is not love, but disobedience and lust as well as low esteem of their own race. It is the love of the flesh and not the love of God. For again, obedience is worth more than any sacrifice you can make, and since women are more gullible than men and men are more easily seduced by women, the sin of interracial marriage increases. Remember, God did not create a half-breed, that is man's idea and doing, not God's.

PROFESSING JESUS, BUT NOT POSSESSING

Over the years and especially in the upcoming presidential election, there are many claims by the Democratic Party that they have Jesus as their Lord and Savior, and no other group of people or party can claim that they have more exclusive rights to him as their Lord than they can have.

The truth of the matter is that any group of people such as the Democratic Party, Liberal Party, or any other organization that supports or condones laws that crush babies' skulls, have babies injected with a fluid to destroy and burn their bodies while they are being formed in a woman's womb, or have the babies' brains sucked out of their skull with a needle and in their total ignorance think Jesus would accept them in any way without repenting sincerely for the murders they have committed, only show how they believe their own lies, because they follow the father of all lies, the Devil. Thus making them children of the Devil (Matthew 13:36-43).

Jesus tells us in Matthew 19:18 to do no murder. Destroying babies in the womb is murder, plain and simple, for it is written, the Lord said he knew you before he formed you and before you came out of the womb. We read in Timothy 2:15, "that the woman is saved in childbearing," not in child or baby killing. Every woman who has an abortion, and who can have a child, is nothing more than a murderer, and will be judged by Jesus as such. Jesus tells us in Matthew 18:6 that if you offend any child in his name that a millstone should be tied around your neck and drown you in the depth of the sea. If this is Jesus' judgment on offending the children, how much more will his judgment be on those that murder babies in the womb? For anyone to think that Jesus would accept your prayers or hymns only shows your total ignorance of him and his righteousness, and all that support abortion, "this is my Savior Jesus; <u>not yours</u>" answer to all of you, when you claim you all know and believe in His name. "I never knew you; depart from me, ye that work iniquity!" "<u>Without repentance and stop what you are doing wrong</u> <u>there is no Forgiveness.</u>"

Many of these same people who support homosexuals, gay marriage, or permit adoption of children by the homosexual society do so, so that they can adopt these young children and seduce them into their lifestyle. Then when they have been abused and brainwashed, send them out to youth groups and schools to recruit more young children into their lifestyle, they will receive the greater damnation, not only those that perform these acts of sodomy on children, but all those people who vote for and support politicians who believe in and enforce the laws of homosexuality and gay marriage.

Jesus tells you he hates the sin of homosexuality, which he states in Rev. 2:6. Nicolaitan teachers are nothing more than mixing God's word with man's word to get people to listen to you who love to have things your way, not God's. Jesus tells us also in Matthew 6:18, He did not come to destroy the Law of God, but to fulfill it and that Heaven and Earth will pass, but not one part of the law will pass away.

If the Father's law in Leviticus 20:13 says that homosexuality is an abomination, and no abomination shall enter into His Kingdom, he means it! And yes! you ignorant so-called scholars, that means all abominations that have not been removed by Christ's grace. For this abomination of homosexuality is still in force, for we read in Romans 1:26 and 27, Paul instructs the people that these lesbians (vs. 26) and male homosexuals (vs. 27) have been turned over to vile affections and degrading passions by God himself, because they changed the truth of God into a lie (Romans 1:25). Paul then tells us in Romans 1:32 that they are worthy of death and all those who approve, vote for, or applaud anyone who supports their lifestyle.

So, am I better than any of these people? <u>Yes! I surely am,</u> and all that worship the Father in Spirit and Truth are. For it is written, the Lord said, Deuteronomy 7:6, "For thou art an holy people unto the Lord they God, The Lord thy God hath chosen thee <u>to be a special people unto</u> <u>himself, above all people that are upon the Face of the Earth!</u>" For abortionists and homosexuals, it is written in Matthew 13:38-40, they are the tares which are the Devil's children, which will be gathered and burned in fire.

Right now, this nation is going through much tribulation, which will only increase in famine, plagues, and death unless there is a full repentance of what the leaders of this country are allowing the Devil's children to do and so-called lazy Christians to start standing up and make a stand for the Lord and not themselves and their so-called comfortable lifestyles. The churches called by Jesus' name are full of Tiny Tim preachers, who tiptoe through the tulips with their Gospel of Love, peace, joy, prosperity, self-esteem, and "God loves you just the way you are" messages, which is the same message as Jim and Tammy Baker brought to the Body of Christ and it failed. For we are not sanctified in Love, we are sanctified in Truth, for the world has Love (John 15:19), but it does not or cannot have the Truth (John 14:17). Sad to say many, many churches have fallen away from the truth, because of their compromising Gospel to please people and make them feel comfortable.

Remember this well, if you don't pick up your Cross and follow him through all he went through and what you will have to go through, you will not have part in his Glorious resurrection. Many are called, but few are chosen.

All you Democrats, Liberals, or any other group that supports or votes for anyone that legislates or enforces laws for abortion or homosexuality are of the same Christian spirit that another leader who claimed what he was doing was for mankind. Adolf Hitler, Hitler murdered millions of people saying they were inferior, just like Democrats and Liberals say the baby in the womb is nothing more than a fetus or glob of flesh, and even though the fetus can move on its own, you Democrats and Liberals, like Hitler, have judged what life is worth living, and what life can be destroyed. The only difference between Democrats, Liberals, and

Hitler is that the Democrats have murdered millions more than Hitler ever did.

For the Spirit of Whoredoms have seduced the people and caused them to error and to go a whoring from under their God. For the heads of the nations have all become sick and have embraced Evil and called it Good, and I will not have mercy on her children, for they are the children of Whoredoms. Thus saith the Lord.

You Democrats and Liberals complain about the war and the thousands of American soldiers that have died there, yet you don't complain about the millions of babies that you have killed through abortion, you hypocrites you! You say that the Lord God does not like wars, you blind leaders and guides, you will be involved with wars and in wars till the end of time. Jesus said in Matthew 24:6, ye shall hear of wars and rumors of wars and nation will rise up against nation. No nation or people will be able to stop wars, they have been here from the beginning and will be around till the end of time. The only person to bring peace to the Earth is Jesus Christ, when he comes back for his people. In the meantime, it is written, "The Lord is a man of war; the Lord is his name" (Exodus 15:3). It is written Exodus 17:16: "The Lord will have war" (Revelation 19:11). Jesus judged and makes war.

It is written, for there fell down many slain because, the war was of God. I Chronicle 5:22: Your only hope is that God is on your side through all the wars you will go through, till he sends his son Jesus to establish peace.

The conclusion of this whole matter is that no one that supports abortion, homosexuality, or legislators that are in favor of it in any form or way will never, ever come into a relationship with Jesus, no matter how much they profess it. And you so-called Christians who are Democrats or Liberals and say you don't believe in abortion or gay marriage, but say there are good things your Democratic leader is going to do, so you vote for this person knowing full well he or she supports gay marriage, the Homosexual Agenda, and abortion, you will be judged with the same doctors that butcher and murder these babies in and out of the womb. You will not be exempt, a little leaven spoils the whole loaf and your righteousness is like filthy rags in God's eyes.

Since so many Christians have been programmed that judging is only for God, I have been instructed to share these words that He has given to me to share with you for your betterment.

To Judge – II Chronicles 19:6, 7

Men called by the Lord to judge not for man but for the Lord, who is with these men in their judgments. For true men called by the Lord to judge, they judge for the Lord not to please men, for they are to be no respecter of persons, or taking of gifts.

To Judge - Jeremiah 5:1

The Lord tells you to run through the streets of his city, seek out if you can find <u>a man</u> (not a group of men) that can executeth judgment that seeks the truth, and then he will pardon it.

To Judge - John 7:24

Jesus said: Judge not according to the appearance, but <u>judge</u> righteous judgment.

To Judge - John 8:26

Jesus said: I have many things to say and to judge of you.

To Judge - John 9:39

Jesus said: For judgment I am come into this world.

To Judge - Matthew 7:1-5

Jesus tells us not to judge when there is a beam in our own eye, but to cast out our beam first, then go to cast out the beam in thy brother's eye. No man is allowed to judge when he has a transgression against God in his soul, that is why only men whose hearts are perfect before the Lord and without fault in his eyes <u>will do judging in his name</u> which are <u>very, very few indeed</u>. The heart can be perfect before the Lord, but the flesh is not. A man without fault is one who will never compromise the word of God for acceptance, and acceptance is 90% of what the men preaching today strive for. They will preach anything that will bring numbers into their churches. <u>Milk</u> is easy to swallow and easy to preach.

To Judge - I Corinthians 2:15

But he that is spiritual <u>judgeth all things</u> yet he himself is judged of no man.

To Judge - I Corinthians 6:1-8

We are told to judge even the smallest matters among ourselves.

To Judge - Luke 12:57

Jesus said: yea and why even of yourselves, judge ye not what is right.

To Judge - John 5:30

Jesus said: "<u>as I hear I judge and my judgment is just</u> because I seek not mine own will, but the will of the Father which hath sent me." True men of God come judging not for their own will, but for the will of the Father. This calling of judging is given to man from the Lord, and these men are also <u>very, very few indeed</u>. For he also says in John 7:18 these few men are true and no unrighteousness is in them.

To Judge - I Corinthians 10:15

We are told to judge what Paul says.

To Judge - I Corinthians 14:29

We are told to let the prophets speak two or three and <u>let the others judge</u>.

Judging - Psalms 37:28

For the Lord loveth judgment.

Judging - Psalms 33:5

For the Lord loveth righteousness and judgment.

To Judge - Isaiah 59:13-15

After reading verses thirteen and fourteen, we read in verse fifteen that it displeased the Lord that there was no judgment. These three scriptures clearly point out how truth has failed in the Lord's churches because people listen to milkmaid preachers and run from and cast out true men called by the Lord to judge.

Judging - Proverbs 19:28

An ungodly witness scorneth judgment, and the mouth of the wicked devoureth inequity.

Judging - Proverbs 21:3

To do <u>justice</u> and <u>judgment</u> is more acceptable to the Lord than sacrifice.

Judging - I Kings 8:32

God tells his servant to judge thy servants condemning the wicked and justifying the righteous.

There are many more instructions from the Lord on judging, and yes, the Lord is the final Judge on all things we do, but he also sends his men to judge matters among his people. The Word of God is full of men he has sent to judge their ways and their nations. As his words were sent to my brother Ezekiel in his writings from the Lord in Ezekiel 2:3-10, so has he sent the same message to my spirit.

Psalms 119:65-72

Is my prayer to the Lord thanking him for teaching me good judgment.

Remember this well, God will not send his men with his judgment to his people from any denomination which is under the control of men, there will be few men who are independent of any Christian organization or leadership. These few men will be judging his people until the Lord God will bring down his final judgment. The Lord always sends a man to warn his people before he judges, for judgment will first start at the House of God. But as always, His people love flattery and milk teachings more than rebuke of their errors.

SERMON ON THE MOUNT
FOR GOD'S PEOPLE,
NOT THE PEOPLE OF THE WORLD

Luke 6:27 and 28

(27) But is said unto you whom hear, "Love your enemies, do good to them that hate you. (28) Bless them that curse you, and pray for them which despitefully use you."

Who is the enemy Jesus is talking about? The enemy Jesus is talking about are <u>his own people,</u> it is not any of the gentile world's people. We read in Matthew 10:36 and a man's foes (enemy) shall be they of his own household. After the sermon on the mount he tells his disciples in Matthew 10:5, "Go not into the way of the gentiles and into any city of the Samaritans, enter ye not but go rather to the lost sheep of the house of Israel." Just like today's Christians argue and fight with each other, so did they in Christ's day, thus becoming their own worst enemies.

Jesus came to unite them into one family by praying and submitting one to another in their faults and hatred towards each other. Jesus said in John 17:9, "I pray for them, <u>I pray not for the world,</u> but for them which thou hast given me." So when we read in Luke 6:28 "pray for them which despitefully use you," he is praying for the Jews that are lost sheep of the house of Israel, just like today we pray for the backsliders and lost Christians in the body of Christ.

Jesus was not or does not pray for anyone of the world as we read in Matthew 13:38. Jesus nowhere prays for the tares, which we read in this verse. In Matthew 4:8 and 9 the Scripture points out to us that the Devil owns and rules the world. "Again the Devil taketh him up into an exceeding high mountain and showed him <u>all the</u> <u>kingdoms of the world</u> and the glory of them, and said unto him, all these things will I give unto thee, if thou will fall down and worship me." Jesus never said they were not his to give, so if he prayed for the world and its kingdoms he would be praying with and for the Devil!

We read then in John 17:20, Jesus says he now prays not only for those whom the Father has given him, but also for them which shall believe on him through the words of his disciples. That is why we are to take his Gospel to all the world so that the people of the world can never say they did not know or hear the word. Then Jesus tells us in Matthew 10:14 and 15, "And who so ever shall not receive you, nor hear your words when ye depart out of that house or city, 'Shake the dust off your feet, verily, I say unto you, it shall be more tolerable for the land of Sodom and Gomorrah, in the day of judgment than for that city.'" This teaching fits perfectly in explaining the Scripture in II Chronicles 19:2, "<u>Shouldest thou help the ungodly, and love them</u> <u>that hate the Lord, therefore is wrath upon thee from</u> <u>before the Lord.</u>"

Christians foolishly pray for heathen nations and their children simply out of a command from their denomination, pastors, or other foolish teachers who are telling them to pray for worldly people and perverted people without first taking them the Gospel of Christ to either accept or reject. For it is written in Romans 8:26, "For we know not what we should pray for as we ought; but the spirit maketh intercession for us with groanings which cannot be uttered. We are to pray against people and nations, as well as we are to pray for them. But only as the spirit leads us, not the way man leads us.

Jeremiah 7:16, Jeremiah 11:14, Jeremiah 14:11, and Psalms 109 are just a few of the Scriptures that tell us to pray against people as well as for them. There is a time when God gets weary with the repenting of his people as we read in Jeremiah 15:6, "Thou art gone backward, therefore I stretch out my hand against thee and destroy thee." "<u>I am weary with repenting.</u>" It is written in 1 John 2:15, "<u>Love not the world, neither the things that are in the world</u>." If any man love the world the love of the Father is not in him. James 4:4: "Know ye not that the friendship of the world is enmity with God? Whosoever therefore will be <u>a friend of the world</u> is the <u>enemy of God</u>." Again this makes more clearly of what Jesus said in John 17:9 and 20.

Do not listen to foolish denominations, pastors, or teachers who take the word <u>world</u> and through their own ignorance try to use it all different ways to support their foolish teachings. These blind guides love to use the Scripture; John 3:16, "For God so loved the world," but it was an ultimatum: Believe in his son Christ, or be condemned. God's love was that he sent his son, the world's love was that they killed his son, thus the words are written after the world killed God's son, "If any man loves the world the love of the Father is not in him."

Jesus tells us in Matthew 25:34 - 46, "All the things you should do for the brethren." In verse 40, he tells us all the things to do for the <u>brethren,</u> not the world. Matthew 12:48, 49, 50; Mark 3:33, 34, 35; and Luke 8:21, Jesus tells who are his and your brethren.

Remember this, that the saying of "hate the sin, love the sinner" pertains only to God's people, not the people of the world, whom Jesus has told you to kick the sand from your sandals, who would not listen to the Gospel and the words of salvation. For the <u>Lord</u> had <u>chosen</u> <u>us</u> to be <u>a special people</u> <u>unto</u> <u>himself</u> <u>above all people that are upon the face of the Earth</u> (Deut. 7:6). Yes, we are above all other people on the Earth, but yet we are a servant to them all, until they reject the Gospel. And to say that God loves a person of the world as much as his own is a lie, and is a saying used by Satan to have you pray for and fellowship with his children so that he eventually can use his subtilty to destroy you.

Yes, we are all part of God's creation, the good and evil, Isaiah 45:7, but we <u>are definitely not all children of God (Matthew 13:38)</u>.

DEMOCRATS AND LIBERALS
HAVING THE HABITS OF CANNIBALS

When you hear of these Democrats and Liberals, Nancy Pelosi and Little Boy Chuckie Schumer say that they believe God, their faith is truly pathetic and pitiful. Do they think that God would listen to their prayers after murdering millions of babies through abortion, and recently discovering bags of babies that were aborted, steam cooked, and tossed in the trash is nothing more than an act of cannibalism! It would be no surprise if they decided to have a cookout if they knew it would give them more votes!

It is written in history, God's people did not remove the heathens that came to them by calling them immigrants and they mingled themselves amongst God's people by using "We are all equal." They started to dismantle God's laws and institute their beliefs and religion among God's. For this is a true saying, God's laws are all equal but God says that the people's ways were unequal (Ezekiel 18:25-29). That murdering babies and steam cooking their bodies are in any way acceptable to the Lord God only shows your height of stupidity and ignorance in all that support and elect these cannibals to office will be judged. The same as those people who abort them and steam cook their young bodies. Your ignorant sayings of "I believe in a woman's right to choose," but not in what they do with the butchered bodies. Anyone who voted for a Democrat or Liberal is as guilty as those murderers that performed these vile deaths! For knowing that the judgment of God on them which commits such things are worthy of death, not only who do the same but have support as pleasure in them that do such things. The Nazis during WWII operated and experimented on Jews, burned and gassed them to death. Democrats and Liberals approved of surgical removal of babies' organs to sell and steam cook their bodies, YOU be the judge. Which is the most heinous?? This is one time you can use your foolish teaching on equality, they both deserve the same judgment with no respect of persons in that judgment of God. Those who vote for these people will only end up finally destroying their own families and loved ones as written in Rev. 2:20-23, rebuke these people and God will bless with Rev. 2:24-26 and keep you free from Deuteronomy 28:61.

If any person or minister says we shouldn't demonize anyone, they are ignorant and blind of God's word, a demon is an evil spirit of a person or thing regarded as cruel. These people of ministers have no meat, just milk, which they're all drowning in. If you don't think that anyone who would believe or legislate in selling baby parts and steam cooking these babies' bodies aren't possessed with evil demons, you truly are lost. Jesus and God speak against evil spirits or demons too many times to count.

Finally I write to tell you I do not like Nancy and Chuckie Boy! I hate them with a perfect hatred. Psalms

139:21-22 Yet I still love them, which many of you will not understand because I still know that God will forgive them if they truly repent. But, if they don't repent my hatred for them is justified and steadfast.

Right now the Boy Scouts and Girl Scouts are filing bankruptcy along with many church organizations because of the homosexuals who were allowed to teach and child molesting that happened there because of these homosexuals, all those Supreme Court justices will be held responsible for these child molesters. They are justified and because of their foolish and ignorant preaching, they have allowed this nation to deteriorate as it has, because the leaders are not involving their flocks to know what season they are in. Remember this well, when these spiritual men and leaders are deceived, it is because the Lord has deceived them (Ezekiel 14:9), because when his truth was given they were corrupt to speak out against sin and error as they were afraid to judge and because of that, the Lord God will judge them and their flocks who listened to those milky messages and those who refused to harken to the meat of the word but wallowed in the milk. Only those who are in the meat of the truth will be found worthy to escape what will be coming to this nation unless there is a change of heart in what they are listening to and then Jesus shall remove those from his Kingdom (reborn Christians) who have offended him because they would not harken unto his truth, only their ways and not his ways! (Matthew 13:41). Unless the churches called by Christ's name speak out and tell the people who they are to vote for and support, these churches will be held accountable for their legislation, and no one will be exempt from that judgment.

WORSHIP IN SPIRIT AND TRUTH

Since the beginning of Jesus Christ's ministry and the Four Gospels were written, Satan started his perverted teachings on love, mixing his love with God's love. Love that millions of Christians and their leaders were deceived into praying and fellowship with Satan and his family where we read about in Matthew 13:36-43 and also in Psalm 58:3. The wicked are hostile (estranged) from the womb speaking lies (tares of Matthew 13:36, soon as they're born). We read in II Corinthians 11:13-15 Satan himself is turned into an angel of light and his murdering and lying family transforms themselves into ministers of righteousness. Satan knows all about God's laws and commandments and his love, for we read in Matthew 4:6 he said it is written if Jesus would cast himself down from the pinnacle of the temple God's angels would not let him be hurt. Jesus answered, "It is also written thou shalt not temp the Lord thy God." So both Satan and Jesus were quoting God's word clearly showing Satan knows Scripture.

There are many kinds of Love but only <u>one Truth,</u> and that's Jesus Christ. Jesus tells us in John 14:6 that He is the truth and the life and no man cometh to the

Father except through Him. You cannot put love before the truth like most churches do, because Jesus and his Father did not command or instruct us to do so. Religious leaders will preach continually on Love because it is easy to do compared to speaking on truth because it divides people and many do not like the sword of God's word as it pierces to the marrow of their bones, and it doesn't go along with the peace they want in their lives. Jesus said in Matthew 10:34, "Think not that I have come to send peace on Earth; I come not to bring peace but a sword." There are many kinds of love, but only one truth. Another kind of love is written about in Timothy 1:6-10, the love of money, it's the root of all evil, clearly showing that this kind of love is evil. Christians are to love people called by God and those who listen to the Word of God. There is nowhere that the truth is called the root of all evil. You must have love, God's love, not the world's, to worship the Father and Son. For it is God's true believing people that have been drawn by God to Jesus, not by religious men.

Remember this well, the Truth sanctifies love, Love does not, nor can it sanctify the Truth. John 17:17: Jesus said, "We are sanctified in the Truth." He does not say in Love; again you cannot put Love before Truth because the Father and Son did not command or instruct us to do so. Truth and Love do go hand in hand but it is a gift from the truth (Jesus). Love is not a gift to justify the Truth, for there are many forms of love, but only one Truth (Jesus).

This is what's in so many of our churches called by Christ's name, a mixture of Satan's love mingled with God's love. For Jesus said in John 4:24, "God is Spirit, and those who worship him must worship him in Spirit and truth." This was a command, not a request. If Jesus had wanted the people to worship the Father in Love he would have said so, but he knew even in his time on Earth there were many many people worshipping God their way and NOT God's way, and that's what's happening in many churches called by Christ's name today.

Many of our churches and their leaders just tell their flocks to just love God with your whole heart, mind, and soul, and you will be alright. Yes, love God with your whole heart, mind, and soul, but if your love is out there before the truth you are disobedient to his order and command, and disobedience is worse than anything you can sacrifice to him. Why have so many Christians been deceived since the writing of the Gospels? Because it is also written in II Corinthians 11:13-15, Satan himself transforms into an angel of light and his murdering and lying family transforms themselves into ministers of righteousness and they use their father's (Satan) and Christ's mixed love message to deceive millions of Christians and their leaders more today than ever. Remember that the person talking and smiling to you in so-called love will easily stab you in the back than a man telling you to repent. In John 14:17 Jesus tells us the world (the tares) receives from their Father's (Satan) love, his love. Jesus tells us how the world loves their own, telling us clearly that the tares and their leaders love their own and use that love to deceive God's people and hate to hear the truth because they can't receive it (John 14:17). Also, it is written how Christians are to fellowship and take the Gospel to the lost and if they listen then stay and fellowship with them, if they do not receive you and the Lord's word then shake the dust off that city and yourself, it will be more terrible for that city than it was for Sodom. As it says in I John 2:15-17, "Love not the world (tares) or the things of the world. If anyone loves the world then the love of the Father is not in them." James 4:4: "Friendship with the world, you become an enemy of God." Any man or woman who tries to convince you that what the Lord has given me is out of context, it is those people that are the deceivers that the Lord has turned over to believe their own lies and as the Pharisees and Scribes in Jesus' day boasting themselves to be wise they have become fools.

It is written John 5:22-27, God the Father will judge no man but committed all judgment unto the son, and has given him authority to execute judgment.

Also we read in I Timothy 2:5, "There is only one mediator between God and mankind, the man Christ Jesus" (the TRUTH). Remember, Love doesn't always come with an olive branch, but also comes with a sword. Jesus said in Matthew 10:34, "Do not think that I have come to bring peace to the Earth, I come not to bring peace but a sword." The churches and their leaders tell you to pray for your enemies and to love your neighbor. But, they don't have the discernment to tell you who your enemies are. Matthew 10:36, Jesus tells you that a man's foes (enemies) will be of his own household. The world (tares) are the Christians' natural enemies. But the deceived Christians that believe in Jesus Christ are the ones in his own household (homes and churches) that have become his new enemies. It wasn't the worldly leaders who condemned Christ to death, for it was God's own people who when the worldly leader Pilate gave them the choice to free Barabbas or Jesus they chose Barabbas. Pilate then said you made your choice, as he was washing his hands he said, "I'm innocent of the blood of this just person" (Matthew 27:24-25). Let his blood be on us (the Jews) and our children. It was Pilate who said to make a sign and put it on the cross, "Jesus of Nazareth, King of the Jews," and when the chief leaders told him to take it down, Pilate said, "What I have written, I have written" (John 19:18-22). It was Pilate who professed Jesus King of the Jews and had it written out for all God's people to see. Jesus did not have to forgive Pilate for his death on the cross, for Pilate found no fault in Him, he gave God's people a choice and they chose to crucify Jesus. So when Jesus said, "Forgive them, Father, for they know not what they do" (Luke 23:34), he was talking to his enemies at the cross and the same enemies who were at the sermon on the mount, his OWN people, not the worldly people (the tares), natural enemy.

In love many Christians have been deceived in praying again for the Devil and his children, for Jesus said in John 17:9 he does not pray for the world (tares), he prays only for those that the Father has given him. Who is your family and neighbor?? Jesus tells you his family are those who hear the Word is God and keep it (Luke 8:21, Matthew 12:50). It is written that no man comes to Jesus except the Father draws him (John 6:24). Reciting the sinner's prayer without God drawing you to Jesus is meaningless (Acts 2:47). The Lord added to the church daily such as should be saved. Not by just reciting the sinner's prayer, for those that the Lord adds to the church they will be known by their fruits (Matthew 7:16-23). Unless the Lord's people pray for and receive a discerning spirit, they will be easily deceived.

Remember this well, worshipping God in Spirit and Truth is key to fully opening God's love to us because it is written I John 5:3, "This is the love of God that we keep his commandments," and in John 4:24 his command is "We must worship him in Spirit and Truth," not Spirit and love, because love can deceive many people. Many Christians and their leaders quote John 3:16: "God so loved the world that he sent his son into the world not to condemn the world but through him (the TRUTH) they might be saved." But they forget to quote the rest of the Scripture, "He that believeth not is condemned already." So without Jesus (the TRUTH) God's love is not there.

BEWARE OF B&B'S

I'm writing this letter as the Lord God has instructed me. The B&B's will be referred to as Biden and his bastards. I will refer to Biden and Cuomo, not President or Governor but as men who in the Lord's eyes have become nothing more than bastards, and since they claim to be Christians this message is for them and their followers, and to those who are not Christians you are on your own to believe whatever you choose, for he that believeth not is condemned already (John 3:18).

The Democratic political party is full of white garbage and black trash. The majority of white and black races are decent people that are being controlled by the minority of white and black militants who put the fear of death and retribution in the majority of the people like the Muslim terrorists put in their people, the Nazi Party was good at it and so is this Democratic Party. It is written in your Christian faith. Deuteronomy 23:2: "A bastard will not enter into the congregation of the Lord," you and your followers in the Lord's eyes are all B's. The Lord God that you say you serve has turned you over to the God of this world... Satan, which you and your followers through their own ignorance and lack of knowledge have succumbed to their own lies, making them partners of your evil ways (Romans 1:32). Mr. Biden, since the day you were turned over to Satan he has already destroyed one of your sons because of sexual permissiveness and turned the other into a liar, whoremonger, and drug addict because of you as their role model. Mr. Cuomo, your sinful pride is that you think you are untouchable like your hero, the Teflon Don, Mr. Gottie. As far as your whoremonger sin, the Italian people that voted for you should remove you from office like the Italian people removed Mussolini from office when he refused to step down. Mr. Biden, if you think that you have not been turned over to your worldly God Satan, just take a good look at yourself and your family in a mirror and see the mental decay of your mind and your family, which will become more frequent unless you repent and make an alliance with President Trump, then the Lord God will bless you both together, but only pride will keep you from that blessing. You and yours cannot hide behind that foolish belief that you are children of the Lord God like your spiritual whore colleague Nancy Pelosi and her sidekick Chuck Schumer.

(1) If you and your B&B's think that you can remove babies from their mother's womb, sell their body parts, steam cook their bodies, put them in bags, and have them dumped in a landfill like it was discovered in Ohio and who knows how many more landfills and still think the Lord our God would call you his child, truly is sad to see such stupidity, but your father the Devil

says, "Well done, good and faithful servant."

(2) As well as allowing homosexuals to be leaders in youth groups like the Boy Scouts and lesbians to be leaders in the Girl Scouts and youth groups and because of your laws that were passed to allow these sexual predators to be put in leadership roles, both the Boy Scouts and Girl Scouts had to file bankruptcies from all the sexual lawsuits caused by these deviates that have physically and mentally maimed these children for the rest of their lives. Putting homosexuals in charge of any youth group is a green light for them to recruit and push their lifestyles since they are parasites and must live off of young people. They can't multiply unless they go to sperm banks of agencies where they can adopt children and then because of these laws allow them to recruit and bring children into their lifestyles, it's like putting a fox in a chicken coop and think that nothing will happen.

(3) Putting multi-gender bathrooms in schools, stores, and places of employment that will only increase sexual promiscuity.

(4) Allowing women to change their sex to a man and a man changing his sex to a woman only shows how sick and depraved you have become.

Now, the Lord and I will clear up some of the foolish teachings that you counterfeit Christians believe in…

(1) We are all equal—UNTRUE (Ezekiel 18:25-32), twice God tells his people his ways are equal, but in his eyes all the people's ways are unequal. Satan likes Christians to believe we are all equal so he can bring in his children to mix and mingle with God's children to see how many he can pull away with his worldly love. John 15:19 tells you that the Devil has love for his children and he uses them to deceive God's children with his love. That is why it is also written, I John 2:15: "Love not the world," also the Gospel of John 17:9 tells you that Jesus does not pray for the world but for those that are his. Psalm 58:3: the wicked are estranged (hostile attitude) from the womb, they go astray as soon as they are born speaking lies. These are Satan's children born of his children's seed and womb.

(2) Once saved always saved— another foolish teaching which is making Christians lost and many self-righteous. For it is written, Hebrews 6:4-6, it is impossible for those who are partakers of the Holy Ghost and made known the good word of God if they should fall away, to bring them back to God would be an open shame. Acts 5:1-11: Ananias and Sapphire believers who lied to God and received death, not forgiveness.

(3) God loves you unconditionally— FALSE. Hebrews 6:4-6, Acts 5:1-11: for the love of God is to keep his Commandments and the 10 Commandments are all conditions. For it is written, obedience is worth more than anything you can sacrifice.

The Lord God is not a Sugar Daddy but you and the Democratic Party have allowed the enemies of the Lord to come into a country under disguise of love and financed and supported them in running for public office that they have grown into great termites that are determined to destroy the foundation of this nation, allowing millions of immigrants to come into the United States who can neither read, write, nor even speak English so that these B&B's can control them with SSI, food stamps, and healthcare. Unless refugees come into this country not like the criminal lawbreakers and use their children as pawns to justify their criminal behavior, they must be treated like the criminals that they are. When these parents say that they want their children to have a better life and send them hundreds of miles to a foreign country that they have never been to and to trust gangsters with their children, it's like putting them in a pit full of rattlesnakes and then they think that they will be alright. Gangsters only recruit to make slaves and gangsters for their own purpose and they love the children to use these parents who send their children hundreds of miles alone, shows that they care not for their safety, but are in fear of their own lives with the belief if they pay and obey that these gangsters of their country will take care of them.

Mr. Biden, to you and your B&B's, please don't say the foolish saying that the Statue of Liberty is for all who seek freedom and liberty. Yes, that it true, it's only a well-meaning proverb, it's not the law of the United States. To receive Liberty and Freedom you must first obey the laws of the nation, with no respecter of persons in the judgment. When you receive money and goods without work, it only makes you a lazy, unproductive person. It is written, II Thessalonians 3:10: "If any would not work, neither shall he eat." Just taking handouts brings forth spoiled fruit and is useless. These words pertain to the healthy, not the afflicted.

Finally, give no room in your life to the B&B's news media, CNN, MSNBC, and all the stations who support Biden and his B's. Propaganda late-night shows like the Johnny Carson wannabes, which are all complete failures and have no talent, but they have been turned over to their own lies that they and their followers believe. Also, there's the trash of CNN news with Chris Cuomo and Don Lemon that make up just a few of the many journalists of that station that are bigots and are prejudice in their intolerance and hatred of other races and creeds. Also, MSNBC with Morning Joe and his sidekicks Rachel Maddox and their journalist on that station, two of the biggest stations of bigots on TV. Then there's the garbage like Maxine Waters, who is truly a bigot and is very ugly too. BLM are all control-freak bigots who push their cause, but it's not for black lives, but for their own political greed and control.... This is just a few of the many groups and people who are doing their best to destroy our American way of life.

Repent and the Lord will truly heal our land (Hebrews 12:7-8).

All you that support the B&B's are as guilty as these B&B's are.

We made the shocking discovery that 44,000 aborted babies from Planned Parenthood abortion clinics were illegally dumped in a Kentucky landfill.

The news came to us through an investigation by then Ohio Attorney General Michael DeWine, whose office exposed that these aborted, murdered babies were steam cooked and tossed in the trash!

WOMAN'S ROLE IN THE CHURCH

In the New Testament we see and read where Jesus called only man to be his apostles, and not one woman and he could have if he choose. Jesus also said, "There is no <u>man</u> that <u>hath</u> <u>left</u> house or brethren or sisters or father or mother or <u>wife</u> or children or lands for my sake and the gospels, shall receive a hundredfold and shall inherit everlasting life" (Matt. 19:29, Mark 10:29, and Luke 18:29). Jesus clearly points out <u>that the man can leave the wife but nowhere does he say the wife can leave her husband to go out and preach his Gospel</u>. Clearly pointed out is the role of the man, and in Titus 2:3, 4, 5, the role of the woman.

Jesus then says in Matt. 13:33 that "the kingdom of Heaven is like unto <u>leaven which a</u> <u>woman took</u> and hid in the three measures of meal, till the whole was leavened." This woman is not the Church, which many blind and foolish ministers proclaim it to be. Jesus tells us clearly in Matt. 16:11 and 12 that the leaven he speaks about is not bread but doctrine. Jesus was not speaking of leaven as doctrine against just the Pharisees and Sadducees, but every time Jesus spoke about leavened he meant doctrines. For we also read in Mark

8:15, Jesus again <u>warns against the</u> <u>leaven of Herod</u>. So we plainly see that when Jesus speaks of the woman in Matt. 13:33 he clearly points out that a woman with just a little leaven (doctrine) can destroy much.

In the New Testament there is <u>no woman preacher, none,</u> there is <u>no woman pastor, teacher, no woman elder</u> or <u>evangelist</u>. There is nowhere a woman delivered any kind of sermon. When these blind pastors and ministers along with the women who bring in the lying spirit that they can also do the roles of men in the Church and you share with them (Tim. 13:12). Deacons must be the husband of one wife, they say that you are interpreting wrong, so they can cover up their sin. When you read them I Timothy 2:11 and 12, women learn in silence and do not teach nor have authority over the man but to be in silence. They again say you are not interpreting correctly and take away from the word and add their own interpretation justly bring on God's judgment on them according to Rev. 22:18-19, Proverbs 30:5-6, and Deut. 4:2. When we read in I Corinth. 14:34-35: "Let the women keep silent in the churches and if they learn anything let them ask their husbands at home, for it is a shame for a woman to speak in the church." When they read this their foolish answers are that this only pertained to the church in Corinth, not to today's church. With that foolish logic, then we can also say that I Corinth. 15:51-57, was it only for the church in Corinth and not for today's church? Many blind guides profess to their flocks that the woman at the well (John 4:6-42) was the first evangelist, because she told the men about Christ, and yet there is no record of her changing her lifestyle or asking for forgiveness. Many Christians today profess Christ as their Lord, but still go on living in fornication and adultery. Then these blind guides again try to point out Mary Magdalene and as the first preacher of the good news because <u>Christ told her to go</u> to my brethren and say unto them, "I ascend unto my father and yours and to my God and your God." Even with the great love Jesus had for Mary, he gave her just one message to take to his brethren, she was never told by Jesus to "go therefore and teach all nations, baptizing them in the name of the Father, Son and Holy Ghost," like he told the men. Then again there is nowhere in the New Testament where any woman baptized, healed, or raised anyone from the dead. And Mary Magdalene is not to be found anywhere in the New Testament in any ongoing ministry. And then there are Aguila and Priscilla, who were always mentioned together, and many so-called Biblical scholars have pointed out that her name sometimes takes precedence over Aquila (Rom. 16:3, Tim. 4:19), when they were called helpers in Christ, and they were saluted along with the household. But these same so-called Biblical scholars fail to tell you that when Apollus was taken aside by Aquila and Pricilla to be explained more accurately the word of God, it was Aquila whose name came first in teaching, not Pricilla. My wife and I share the Gospel with many people in our home, and many say that they are going to go over to my wife's house to hear her husband teach the word along with her, but she is never the teacher; she keeps her role as the Scripture proclaims in Titus 2:3, 4, 5. Then there is Phoebe in Rom. 16:1-2, him again many blind guides call her a deaconess. Yet there is nowhere in the word that Paul called her a deaconess or any woman a deaconess. Phoebe helped Paul in preparing the church at Conchrea, like many women today in the Church prepare the food and arrangements for the coming of the minister or evangelist to speak his sermon. They do not teach alongside of a pastor or minister of the word but do share in the word. And again because the leaders and women in the churches love to have leadership roles without the roles that God has instituted in his word for this cause, God turns them over to believe their own lies and follow not the spirit of truth but the spirit of error, that they might be damned who believe not the truth but have pleasure in unrighteousness.

These people cover up <u>their sins by their worldly Trinity,</u> which is 1) that word doesn't mean that 2) you are not interpreting the word correctly. 3) In the Greek and Hebrew this is what it really means. When these leaders teach all their flock Greek and Hebrew so that they also know what they're saying, then you can start quoting Greek and Hebrew. It's like me reading the word of God in Polish and German and telling the people what I'm saying is true when they don't understand what I'm saying in Polish or German. Galatians 3:28 pertains to salvation only. It doesn't matter who you are, once you accept Jesus Christ as your Lord and Savior you become as one in the body of Christ, but in the body of Christ men and women have different roles to perform for the Lord. The women are to teach the young women to be sober, to love their husbands, to love their children, to be discreet, chaste keepers at home, good, obedient to their husbands, that the word of God be not blasphemed <u>(Titus 2:4-5),</u> Paul then writes in I

Timothy <u>2:11,12,</u> that the women in Christ's church are to learn in silence with all subjection. But I suffer not a woman to teach, nor to usurp authority over the man, but to be in silence. If the Apostle Paul, who wrote Galatians 3:28, meant that a woman could do all that a man could, why then did he write out the duties of what a Godly woman should do and teach in Titus 2:4-5 and then tell her what she should not do in the body of Christ in I Tim. 2:11-12? If it didn't matter what roles women and men should have in the body of Christ, Paul should not have pointed them out so plainly. Either Paul was a <u>doubleminded man, which he was not,</u> or he truly meant that Galatian 3:28 pertained definitely to salvation and not to opening the roles of men and women to do whatever they want in the church. God is a God of order, not confusion.

Finally there's Deborah, a prophetess, the wife of Lapidoth whom many ministers and preachers say she was the judge and leader of the Israel people. Yes, she was a judge but not a leader of the people. Yes, she did give judgment to the children of Israel, but a judge gives you the law and how you must obey it. Yes, there were also men called judges but many of them were warriors along with being judges. Deborah was a woman prophetess who was judging the people of Israel in their lifestyle and living according to the law. She was not a leader but a judge. Even today in any courtroom the judge instructs the law and if the person breaks the law he or she pays the penalty for breaking it. The judge does not lead the people as a king would or shepherd leads his flock. A judge only instructs the law. It's up to the individual or individuals to follow the judge's instructions under penalty of punishment. When

Deborah told Barak he was to go against Jabin's army and his multitude and the Lord would deliver him into his hand, Barak said, "I will go if thou will go with me, if thou will not go with me then I will not go." Barak knew the odds were against him and he knew that if he was losing the battle but was told by Deborah the Lord had commanded it, then according to the law Deborah should be put to death for prophesying a lie in the Lord's name, that is the reason he demanded her to go with him. Deborah also said that the journey he would take would not be for his honor, for the Lord shall sell Sisera into the hand of a woman. That woman was not Deborah, but it was Jael who drove a nail with a hammer through Sisera's head and fastened it to the ground. It was Jael that was called blessed above the women, not Deborah, though she was differently used by the Lord. So to use Deborah as an example that women can be preachers and ministers of God's word only shows how the feminist movement has swept into churches of Jesus Christ after it only says in Scripture that woman are to teach (Titus 2:3-5). There is so much to teach women by women because of the filthy and wickedness of this nation in churches, politics, and entertainment. But as it was in the beginning, so shall it be at the end. A man, Adam, listening to a woman, Eve, telling him what to do. It is written in I Tim. 2:14: "And Adam was not deceived but the woman being deceived was in a transgression." Men must have a discerning spirit to know who to listen to. Many don't.

EXPOUNDING OF GRACE & THE LAW

When Jesus arose from the dead he appeared to the disciples, once when Thomas was absent and once when he was present. It is written that he did many other signs which are not written in this book in the presence of his disciples. John 20:30 and 31, Jesus showed himself again to his disciples at the Sea of Tiberias and dined with them, if Jesus was their Teacher, and the Lord wanted to change any of his Father's laws, he would have told his disciples what laws were no longer to be obeyed. Jesus did not tell them to change his Father's laws, because he had already said, "Think not that I have come to destroy the Law or the prophets, I have come not to destroy, but to fulfill" (Matthew 5:17 and 18). When Jesus died on the cross, the sacrificing of all animals was done away with because he was the final perfect sacrifice and penalties of death and physical punishment for disobedience under the law were forgiven under repentance, grace, and mercy. Jesus was circumcised, dedicated, kept the Sabbath and the Passover, nowhere is there where the Lord did away with any of these laws before he was crucified or after he rose from the dead. He did not come to give us new commandments, just what he said in Matthew 22:36-40. Jesus came to do the will of the Father and not his or any man's will, which he stated in Mark 7:7-9.

When I read and listen to so many of these blind guides who I know many of them love the Lord, but are ignorant of God's word and they harden their hearts when they hear the word of God come to them because they haven't the discernment to know what is truth and what is error. Their teachings on grace, circumcision, Sabbath, and the Passover are just a few of their foolish teachings. I have been instructed to teach those who have an ear to hear and eyes to read those laws which the Lord did not do away with. There are many laws, but the one law which almost all Christian churches have erred and disobeyed God's law is circumcision. Peter and Paul had a head-to-head disagreement on this law. Peter said, "You must be circumcised in the Flesh." Paul said, "You only have to be circumcised in your heart." But, we read in Ezekiel 44:7-9, God said not to bring into his sanctuary any strangers who are uncircumcised in the heart or uncircumcised in the Flesh. So the Lord has already told us before Paul preached on circumcising that the heart along with the flesh was to be circumcised in order to enter into his sanctuary. There is nowhere Jesus changed that law; Paul says in Galatians 2:7 and 8, Peter was given the Gospel of Circumcision and Paul the Gospel of Uncircumcision, this then would show that God is doubleminded, which he is not, it is man who is doubleminded.

To think that God would give a choice to his Church, that one part of the Church must keep his laws and the other Church called by his name does not have to keep it, is totally foolish, which would only create a house that is divided, and Jesus said, "A house divided among itself cannot stand." If in the days of when Peter and Paul were bringing people into the knowledge of Jesus Christ and building churches in His name, common sense would reveal to the men in those days if they wanted Jesus in their lives in Paul's churches, they would not have to be circumcised. It's easy to understand which they would choose, it's one of the reasons Paul built more churches than Peter. Either Peter was right on circumcision or Paul was, they were not both right. God is not the author of confusion, there is nowhere in Scripture that Peter stopped preaching on circumcision or Paul stopped preaching on uncircumcision. Many of these blind guides quote II Peter 3:15 and 16 to mean that Peter changed his mind and accepted Paul's teachings of being uncircumcised. If these blind guides believed that Peter later preached on uncircumcision or accepted it as a teaching, then he was disobeying the Gospel that Paul said was given to him to do (Galatians 2:7-8). God would not allow one to keep his law and the other not to, as this would only lead to confusion. Paul, whom I believe loved the Lord and is with him now, was a man who pleased people, not in all things, but in some.

Jesus said to his disciples, "Go ye therefore and teach all nations, <u>baptizing</u> them in the name of the Father, the Son, and of the Holy Ghost. Teaching them to observe all things whatsoever, <u>I have commanded you.</u>" Jesus' <u>command was to his disciples to baptize them all</u>. Yet Paul says in Corinthians 1:14-17, he was not called to baptize, but Jesus gave a command in

Matthew 28:19 and 20 to baptize. To think that Jesus gave this command and then told one of his men you don't have to follow it is completely foolish and ignorant and again would make Jesus a doubleminded man, which Jesus was definitely not!

It took Jesus over a thousand years to finally correct Moses' manmade law on divorce, which through all the years caused God much heartache. Some of the laws Moses gave to his people were from his own heart, just like Paul gave many liberties to his churches that were from his own heart, not the Lord's, for as much as Paul loved the Lord Jesus, he like all men was not perfect, only Jesus was. For Paul himself admits in Romans 7:15-25 that he does things right and wrong and it's the battle we all have in the Spirit to obey and the Flesh to disobey. Again, the blind guides will quote II Timothy 3:16 and 17, all Scripture is given by inspiration of God and is profitable for doctrine, <u>for reproof, for correction</u>, for instruction in righteousness, and they will quote II Peter 1:20 and 21 knowing this first that no prophecy of the Scripture is any private interpretation, for the prophecy came not in old time by the will of man, but holy men of God who spoke as they were moved by the Holy Ghost. These so-called ministers who use these scriptures to justify their teachings have no knowledge or wisdom from God, only from men who claim to be anointed by the Lord, many of these men truly love the Lord, but again, anointed by men, not the Lord.

Most of these teachers and so-called Biblical scholars sincerely believe in what they are doing to God's word is anointed, but they are <u>sincerely wrong</u>. These "scholars" have changed the word of God so many times since the scriptures went into print, you would need a library to hold them all. There are many examples of man's ignorance to God's word, but I will use man's most recent perversion of God's word, it's called the N.I.V. Bible. When the authors of this so-called Bible met in 1965 to make a new translation of the Bible and invited many denominations to help, it was only inspired by the Flesh, not the Spirit. For <u>I will be blunt, in my judgment of</u> <u>these blind guides</u>, they were no more anointed than a fart in a windstorm, and have become no more than hemorrhoids on the body of Christ. When they published the N.I.V. New Testament in 1973, they found that they had made many mistakes and had to make new corrections and revisions, then yet again had to make corrections and went to print in 1978. Once again, more mistakes and revisions were made and went to print in 1983. When you have to go back year after year to correct what you think God gave you to do the first time, it only shows the Spirit of Truth was not with you, but the Spirit of Error was (John 4:6). When the first N.I.V. came <u>164</u> <u>verses</u> had been changed and altered, as well as omitting the name of the Lord God <u>169</u> times from the New Testament. The word "<u>charity</u>" has been totally <u>removed</u> from the N.I.V. and the word "<u>love</u>" has <u>replaced</u> it instead. What's next for these blind guides, <u>remove grace</u>, put in love, <u>remove mercy</u>, put in love, <u>remove forgiveness</u>, put in love, and the list could go on. <u>All the Gifts of God</u> are love, but when you take away the meaning of the <u>gifts of Love God gives</u>, you lose the meaning of the personal gift he gave you!

In conclusion remember this well, we who are truly in obedience to the Lord <u>are Sanctified in the Truth</u>

(John 17:17-19). There is nowhere we are sanctified in Love. When we speak of Love, it must be God's love because the world and its people have love, which we read in John 15:19, that the world will love his own, so we see the world has love. We read in Matthew 4:8 the Devil showed Jesus <u>all the kingdoms of the world</u> and said, "All these I will give thee," thus clearly showing you the world and its kingdoms are of the Devil, and we have just read in John 15:19 that the world will love its own, and we read the world and its kingdoms belong to Satan, clearly showing that the Devil has his own kind of Love. But one thing that Satan cannot have is the Truth, for Jesus said, "Even the Spirit of Truth whom the world cannot receive" (John 14:17). You must have discernment from God to know of his love and the Love the world has for its own. Satan has been successful in mixing his love with the Lord's and sad to say many Christians have fallen into the snare of his love. That is why Jesus said, we must worship the Father in Spirit and Truth (not Love because God is Love), and we are Sanctified in Truth, not Love (John 4:23 and 24). <u>Finally, know which Love you preach and share whether it be of God and Jesus or whether it be of the world and Satan.</u>

You can take the revelation of God's word, which he has given me to share with his Church, and digest it and bring new life to your soul, or you can spit it out and call it any name you or your leaders want to call and it can be your choice to accept the wormwood of many years of error. And for all the blind guides who have called me a False Prophet or False Teacher, you must prove that I am what you say by the Word of God, not by your own feelings. By your words you will be justified or condemned. I will gladly come anywhere, anytime, and anyplace and let the Lord judge which of us have the truth and which has only man's "teachings" and "doctrines."

THE BLACK-AND-WHITE ISSUE

I am neither Democratic nor Republican nor any race supporter. When dealing with the issue of black and white, that is exactly what I will deal with. When God created the black man, he was created with the gifts of speed and strength. That is why they excel in sports, which demand speed and strength. God created the white man with the gifts of wisdom and knowledge, and that is why this country grew so fast, because of the wisdom and knowledge of the white man. Any contribution made to this country by the black man was because the white man taught him to read and write. This is proven just by looking at Europe and Africa today. Europeans have advanced in all fields of health, science, inventions, and the best living conditions. The blacks in Africa are still the same as they were thousands of years ago, and if it wasn't for the white man teaching blacks, they would still be living in the jungles as they are still doing today. When the blacks cry about the slavery issue, they must remember that it was their own black chiefs in Africa who sold them to the white man, making them just as guilty as the white men who bought them.

The white man didn't need affirmative action to get them jobs, but because of the lack of wisdom and knowledge, the black man again went to the white politicians and cried out for fairness and justice, so that the black people who could not pass the aptitude test would get jobs that the people with a higher I.Q. should receive.

The black race will not let go of the slavery issue, which is a horrible stain on this country, like the mistreatment of the Indians by the white man, whose country this first belonged to. But you don't see the Indians continually hollering racism if issues don't go their way. They have learned to live and govern among themselves through many of the problems that they have had to face.

REMEMBER THIS WELL:

1) When you drive your car, thank the white man.

2) When you fly in an airplane, thank the white man.

3) When you go into a supermarket, thank the white man.

4) When you watch a football, baseball, or basketball game, thank the white man.

5) When you go to the phone, stove, refrigerator, or television, again thank the white man.

WISDOM
GOD'S DELIGHT AND CHRIST'S MOTHER

We read in Matt. 11:19, Jesus calls himself a <u>child of wisdom</u> and then again he says in Luke 7:35, "<u>wisdom is justified of all her children</u>." To understand these two verses we first must read Proverbs 8:22-36, which tell us how God possessed wisdom in the beginning of his ways before his works of old. <u>She</u> was his delight and was brought up with him from the beginning when the Earth came to be. He prepared the heavens, I was there. We read in John 17:24, Jesus said the father loved Jesus before the foundation of the world. When God possessed wisdom in the beginning of his ways is when he brought forth Jesus and many other sons of God, who were with him when he said in Genesis 1 vs. 26 and 27, "Let <u>us</u> make a man in our image after <u>our</u> likeness, in the image of God created he him, male and female created he them." We read in Job 1-6 there were many spirited sons of God, we've read in Proverbs beside wisdom being what we would called female, there are also many other female spirits in Proverbs 7:4 understanding female spirit. I Corinth. 13:5 charity called her, James 1:4 patience called her. We read in

Lamentations 1 through 5 that Judah and Jerusalem are called she and her and the daughter of Zion called her, which clearly points out the family of God and wisdom. Jesus' spiritual mother was wisdom, his fleshy mother was Mary. When Jesus was at the wedding feast at Cana, Mary, his fleshy mother, said unto him they have no wine, Jesus answered her not by calling her mother but said to her, "<u>Woman</u>," and when Jesus was on the cross John 19:26, 27, he said to his fleshy mother Mary, who was next to the disciple whom he loved, "<u>Woman,</u> behold thy son and to his disciple behold thy mother." Mary was a fleshy and blessed woman, was used to bring forth his spiritual son to be sacrificed for our sins. Jesus knew his spiritual mother was wisdom and Mary was a blessed woman when God used to bring forth Jesus in the flesh.

Over the last 40 years my Father and Brother, Jesus Christ, my Savior, with the Holy Spirit, especially the last five years, had me write letters to the churches called by his Name, to the Leaders of America to the churches about their lack of truth, knowledge and Wisdom. They had rejected the messages and continued to worship God & Jesus Christ as their "Sugar Daddy." The Leaders of America and their followers now from year 2022 on their filthiness, rebellion and lying will be judged by words the Lord has given me and those that profess Christ as their Lord that are among them but show their alliance to these Murderers, Liars, Thieves and every filthy lifestyle even when they knew they slaughtered millions of young babies in and out of the womb. The word tells you that from the richest, poorest, and greatest from the prophets and priests that dealeth falsely with these evildoers and were not ashamed. The Lord will bring more plagues in this nation and increase sorrow and pain. And the Nations of the North and the East which is a language many do not fully understand shall rise up against thee and your destruction shall not only come from the sky but also from the Great Waters surrounding America. For these Leaders of America glorified themselves and their political party and lived lavishly and deliciously and did not feel they needed their help and guidance from the Lord. And these rich and Greedy people will be among the first to feel the wrath and judgment of God and their money and friends will not help them in their time of judgment. Like the people in Japan were destroyed in many cities during World War II, because of the Warmongering, and power-seeking leaders, they followed and supported that when judgment came that their flesh was consumed away while they stood upon their feet and their eyes shall consume away also while they stand upon their feet and their tongues shall consume away in their mouth and as the Lord used America to destroy the enemies against us in explosive fire he will now use our enemies because we have rejected his teachings and have become vain and prideful in our own ways and allowed the enemy to receive power and authority over us by putting them and electing them to offices of Power and Authority to make their laws and morals over God's and deceive many into their Unholy and Unmoral ways.

The Lord then shall cause a famine in the Land and it shall increase with plagues, and the Lord will cause the people to eat the flesh of their sons and the flesh of their daughters, and they shall eat every one the flesh of their friends because of the War and destruction their enemies brought upon them. And many of the rulers of the World shall see the smoke of her burning and say America, America, that mighty nation for in one hour it was judged by the Almighty God and those whom the Lord found worthy to escape cried to the Lord to spare them that were being judged, but the Lord replied, "I will not answer nor save them in their times of trouble, for through willful sinning they weary me with their fleshly repenting, because it has not come from a righteous heart but a fleshly mind and mouth."

But now I tell you to hold back my hand of judgment to your nation, you must now run through your nation and seek and find a man, not a group of men but a man who will execute judgment and that seeketh the truth and then and only then will I remove my judgment and pardon the people.

Thus saith the Lord…